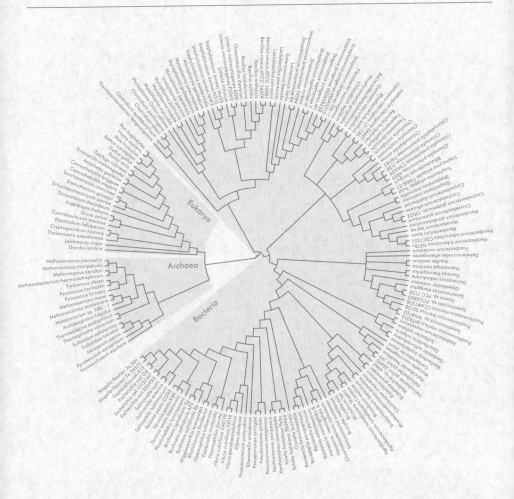

Archaea, constituting the smallest domain of the phylogenetic tree, are prokaryotes: single-cell organisms lacking a nucleus or any membrane-bound organelles. Originally classified as a type of bacteria (archaebacterial), archaea in fact contain rRNA that is unique to them. They have membranes made of branched hydrocarbon chains. Visually, they are closer to bacteria but in their genes and enzymes resemble eukarya. Archaea have a wide range of habitats including extreme environments like hot springs and salt lakes. Their energy sources range from sugars to ammonia and metal ions.

Eukarya are distinguished from the other two domains of the tree by the presence of a nucleus and other membrane-bound cells like mitochondria and the Golgi apparatus. Their membranes are composed of unbranched fatty acid chains. All multicellular organisms fall under this domain, which is subdivided into the kingdoms of Protista (slime molds, algae, protozoans); Fungi (fungi, yeasts, molds); Plantae (mosses, ferns, flowering plants); and Animalia (sponges, worms, insects, vertebrates).

Bacteria—far and away the largest domain of the tree—are made up of prokaryotic cells, like the archaea. Like the eukarya, however, their cell membranes are composed of unbranched fatty acid chains. Bacteria are unique in that their cell walls often contain peptidoglycan, a polymer critical to the survival of many bacteria. One of the first life forms on the planet, bacteria thrive in habitats ranging from soil and water to acidic hot springs, arctic environments, and radioactive waste.

LIFE	DOMAIN	KINGDOM	PHYLUM	CLASS	ORDER	FAMILY	GENUS	SPECIES

	A	B	C	D	E	F	G	H	I	J	K	L	M	N	O
1															
2															
3															
4															
5															
6															
7															
8															
9															
10															

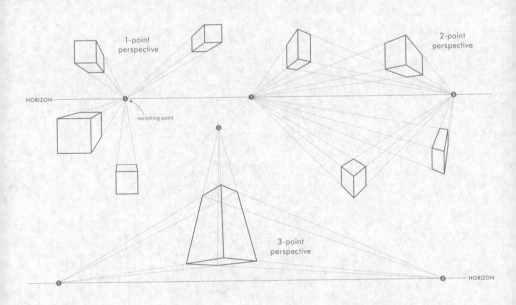

1-point perspective

HORIZON

vanishing point

2-point perspective

3-point perspective

HORIZON

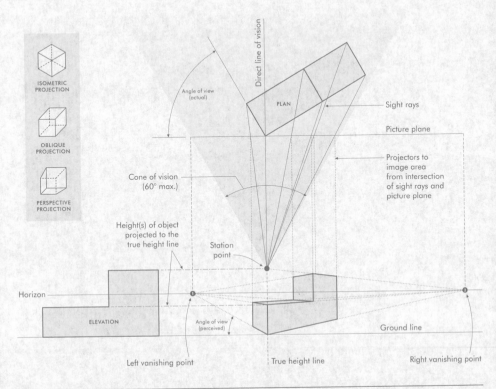

ISOMETRIC PROJECTION

OBLIQUE PROJECTION

PERSPECTIVE PROJECTION

Direct line of vision

Angle of view (actual)

PLAN

Sight rays

Picture plane

Cone of vision (60° max.)

Projectors to image area from intersection of sight rays and picture plane

Height(s) of object projected to the true height line

Station point

Horizon

ELEVATION

Angle of view (perceived)

Ground line

Left vanishing point

True height line

Right vanishing point

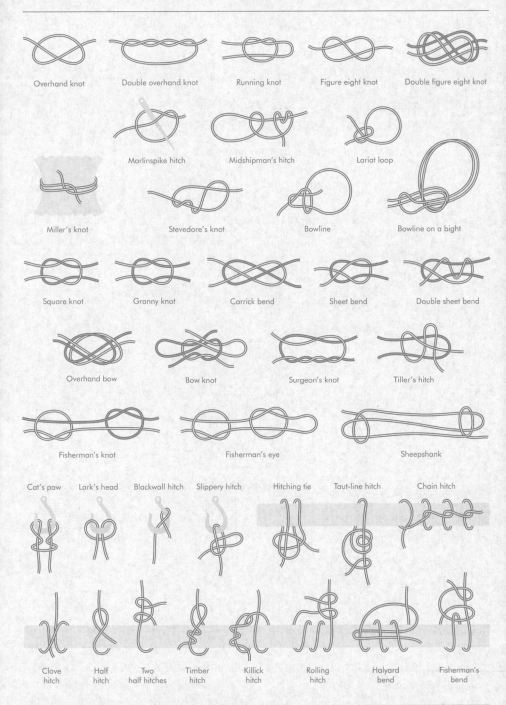

Overhand knot   Double overhand knot   Running knot   Figure eight knot   Double figure eight knot

Marlinspike hitch   Midshipman's hitch   Lariat loop

Miller's knot   Stevedore's knot   Bowline   Bowline on a bight

Square knot   Granny knot   Carrick bend   Sheet bend   Double sheet bend

Overhand bow   Bow knot   Surgeon's knot   Tiller's hitch

Fisherman's knot   Fisherman's eye   Sheepshank

Cat's paw   Lark's head   Blackwall hitch   Slippery hitch   Hitching tie   Taut-line hitch   Chain hitch

Clove hitch   Half hitch   Two half hitches   Timber hitch   Killick hitch   Rolling hitch   Halyard bend   Fisherman's bend

WORLD MAP

+12:00 Auckland

+10:00 Hagåtña, Canberra

+9:00 Seoul, Tokyo

+8:00 Beijing, Taipei,
Hong Kong,
Manila, Perth

+7:00 Hanoi, Bangkok,
Jakarta

+6:30 Yangon

+6:00 Almaty, Dhaka

+5:45 Kathmandu

+5:30 Delhi

+5:00 Tashkent, Karachi

+4:30 Kabul

+4:00 Dubai

+3:30 Tehran

+3:00 Moscow, Baghdad,
Nairobi

+2:00 Helsinki, Istanbul, Athens,
Jerusalem, Beirut, Cairo,
Johannesburg

+1:00 Stockholm, Berlin,
Warsaw, Paris, Vienna,
Rome, Madrid

UTC 0:00 Dublin, London, Lisbon,
Casablanca, Abidjan

−3:00 São Paulo, Buenos Aires

−3:30 St. John's

−4:00 San Juan, Santo Domingo,
La Paz, Santiago

−4:30 Caracas

−5:00 Toronto, New York,
Havana, Kingston,
Bogotá, Lima

−6:00 Chicago, Houston,
Mexico City,
Guatemala City

−7:00 Denver

−8:00 Vancouver, Seattle,
San Francisco,
Los Angeles, Tijuana

−9:00 Anchorage

−10:00 Honolulu

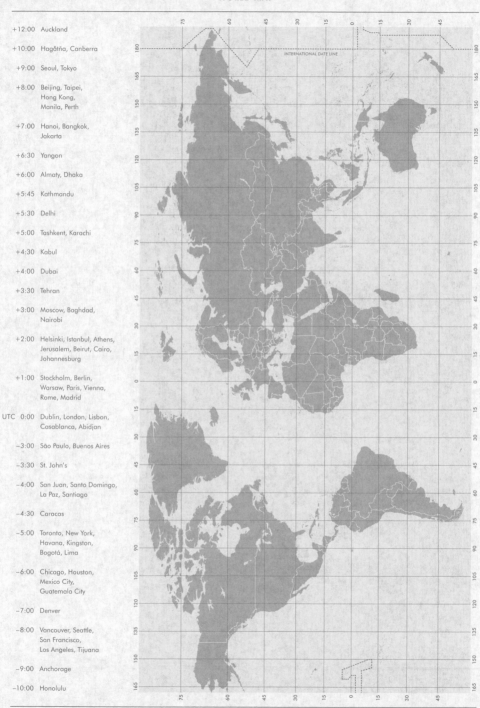

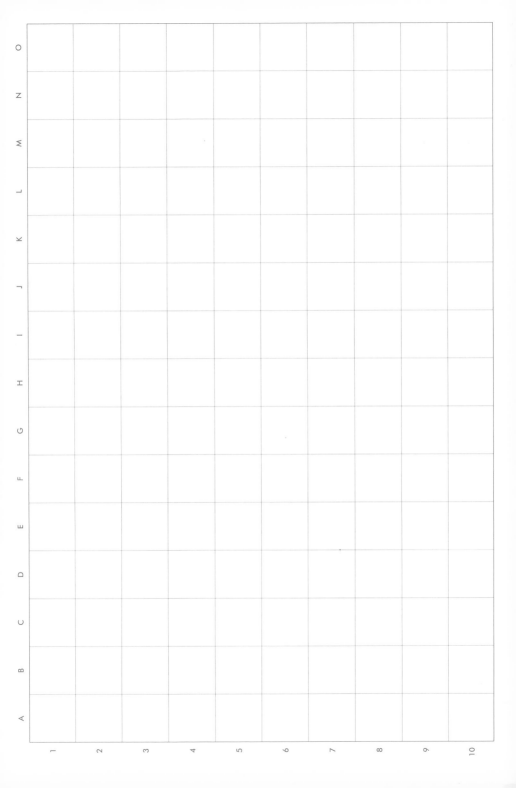

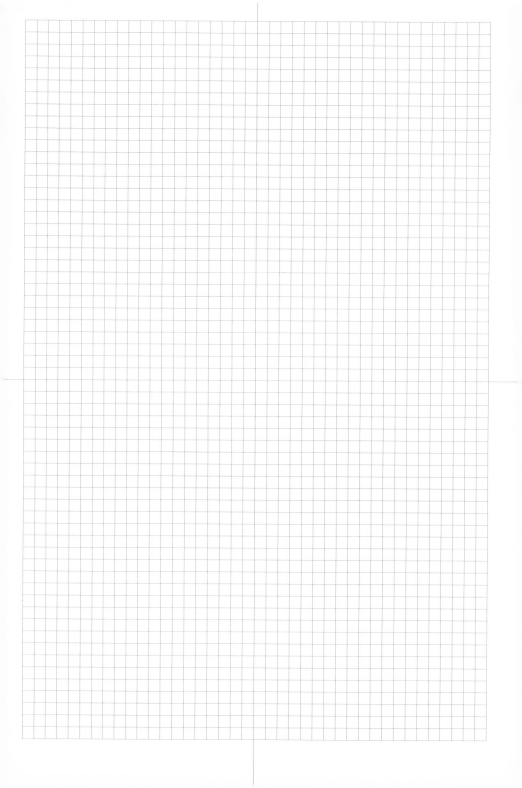

LOGICAL CONNECTIVES

Contradiction (false)

Notation	Formulas	Truth table (Q: 0 1)	Venn diagram	Example
$\perp$ "bottom"	$P \wedge \neg P$ Opq	P 0: 0 0 P 1: 0 0		The moon is out and the moon is not out.

Tautology (true)

Notation	Formulas	Truth table (Q: 0 1)	Venn diagram	Example
$\top$ "top"	$P \vee \neg P$ Vpq	P 0: 1 1 P 1: 1 1		The moon is out or the moon is not out.

Proposition P

Notation	Formulas	Truth table (Q: 0 1)	Venn diagram	Example
P	p Ipq	P 0: 0 0 P 1: 1 1		The moon is out.

Negation of P

Notation	Formulas	Truth table (Q: 0 1)	Venn diagram	Example
$\neg P$ $\sim P$	Np Fpq	P 0: 1 1 P 1: 0 0		The moon is not out.

Proposition Q

Notation	Formulas	Truth table (Q: 0 1)	Venn diagram	Example
Q	q Hpq	P 0: 0 1 P 1: 0 1		I am awake.

Negation of Q

Notation	Formulas	Truth table (Q: 0 1)	Venn diagram	Example
$\neg Q$ $\sim Q$	Nq Gpq	P 0: 1 0 P 1: 1 0		I am not awake.

Conjunction

Notation	Formulas	Truth table (Q: 0 1)	Venn diagram	Example
$P \wedge Q$ $P \& Q$ $P \cdot Q$ $P_{\text{AND}} Q$	$P \nrightarrow \neg Q$ $\neg P \nleftarrow Q$ $\neg P \downarrow \neg Q$ Kpq	P 0: 0 0 P 1: 0 1		The moon is out and I am awake.

Alternative Denial

Notation	Formulas	Truth table (Q: 0 1)	Venn diagram	Example
$P \uparrow Q$ $P \mid Q$ $P_{\text{NAND}} Q$	$P \rightarrow \neg Q$ $\neg P \leftarrow Q$ $\neg P \vee \neg Q$ Dpq	P 0: 1 1 P 1: 1 0		The moon is not out if I am awake.

Disjunction

Notation	Formulas	Truth table (Q: 0 1)	Venn diagram	Example
$P \vee Q$ $P_{\text{OR}} Q$	$P \leftarrow \neg Q$ $\neg P \rightarrow Q$ $\neg P \uparrow \neg Q$ $\neg(\neg P \wedge \neg Q)$ Apq	P 0: 0 1 P 1: 1 1		The moon is out or I am awake.

Joint Denial

Notation	Formulas	Truth table (Q: 0 1)	Venn diagram	Example
$P \downarrow Q$ $P_{\text{NOR}} Q$	$P \nleftarrow \neg Q$ $\neg P \nrightarrow Q$ $\neg P \wedge \neg Q$ Xpq	P 0: 1 0 P 1: 0 0		The moon is not out nor am I awake.

Material Nonimplication

Notation	Formulas	Truth table (Q: 0 1)	Venn diagram	Example
$P \nrightarrow Q$ $P \not\supset Q$	$P \wedge \neg Q$ $\neg P \downarrow Q$ Lpq	P 0: 0 0 P 1: 1 0		Just because the moon is out does not mean I am awake.

Material Implication

Notation	Formulas	Truth table (Q: 0 1)	Venn diagram	Example
$P \rightarrow Q$ $P \supset Q$	$P \uparrow \neg Q$ $\neg P \leftarrow \neg Q$ Cpq	P 0: 1 1 P 1: 0 1		If the moon is out then I am awake.

Converse Nonimplication

Notation	Formulas	Truth table (Q: 0 1)	Venn diagram	Example
$P \nleftarrow Q$ $P \not\subset Q$	$P \downarrow \neg Q$ $\neg P \wedge Q$ $\neg P \nrightarrow \neg Q$ Mpq	P 0: 0 1 P 1: 0 0		The moon is not out but I am awake.

Converse Implication

Notation	Formulas	Truth table (Q: 0 1)	Venn diagram	Example
$P \leftarrow Q$ $P \subset Q$	$P \vee \neg Q$ $\neg P \rightarrow \neg Q$ Bpq	P 0: 1 0 P 1: 1 1		The moon is out if I am awake.

Exclusive Disjunction

Notation	Formulas	Truth table (Q: 0 1)	Venn diagram	Example
$P \nleftrightarrow Q$ $P \not\equiv Q$ $P \oplus Q$ $P_{\text{XOR}} Q$	$P \leftrightarrow \neg Q$ $\neg P \leftrightarrow Q$ $\neg P \nleftrightarrow \neg Q$ Jpq	P 0: 0 1 P 1: 1 0		Either the moon is out or I am awake—never both.

Biconditional

Notation	Formulas	Truth table (Q: 0 1)	Venn diagram	Example
$P \leftrightarrow Q$ $P = Q$ $P_{\text{XNOR}} Q$ $P_{\text{IFF}} Q$	$P \nleftrightarrow \neg Q$ $\neg P \nleftrightarrow Q$ $\neg P \leftrightarrow \neg Q$ Epq	P 0: 1 0 P 1: 0 1		The moon is out if and only if I am awake.

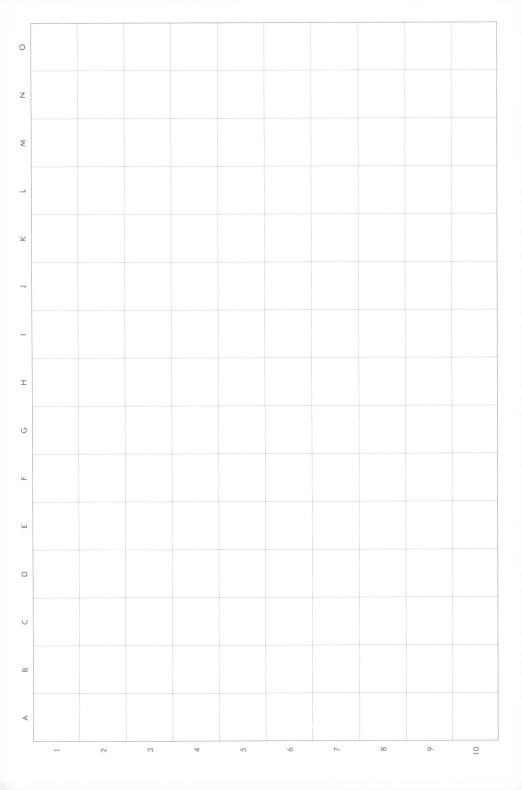

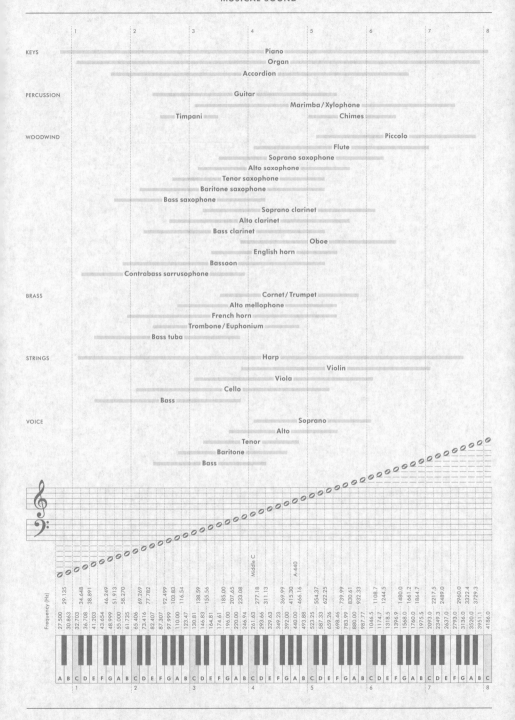

UNIT EQUIVALENTS

TEMPERATURE

Fahrenheit $[°F] = 1.8\,[°C] + 32$ Celsius $[°C] = ([°F] - 32) / 1.8$ Kelvin $[K] = [°C] + 273.15$ Rankine $[R] = 1.8\,[K]$

LENGTH

Symbol	Unit	Equivalent	Equivalent	Notes
pc	parsec	19,173,500,000,000 mi	31,185,000,000,000 km	3.3 light-years
ly	light-year	5,878,500,000,000 mi	9,450,000,000,000 km	63,000 AU
AU	astronomical unit	92,955,700 mi	150,000,000 km	Earth-to-sun distance
	nautical league	18,228.3 ft	5.556 km	3 nautical miles
	statute league	15,840 ft	4.828 km	3 miles
nmi	nautical mile	6,076.12 ft	1.852 km	1 minute of arc (1/60°)
mi	statute mile	5,280 ft	1.60934 km	8 furlongs
	cable	720 ft	219.456 m	120 fathoms
	furlong	660 ft	201.168 m	10 chains
	chain	66 ft	20.1168 m	4 rods
rd	rod	16.5 ft	5.0292 m	25 links
	fathom	6 ft	1.8288 m	2 yards
m	meter	3.28084 ft	100 cm	distance light travels in 1/299,792,458 sec
yd	yard	3 ft	0.9144 m	
ft, ′	foot	12 in	0.3048 m	1/3 yard
	link	7.92 in	20.1168 cm	1/100 chain
in, ″	inch	0.083 ft	25.4 mm	6 picas
pc	pica	0.16 in	4.23 mm	12 points
pt	point	0.0138 in	0.3527 mm	1/72 inch
cm	centimeter	0.393701 in	10 mm	
mm	millimeter	0.0393701 in	0.001 m	1,000 micrometers
	thou, mil	0.001 in	0.0254 mm	
Å	ångström	0.00000000393701 in	0.0000001 mm	0.1 nanometer

AREA

Symbol	Unit	Equivalent	Equivalent	Notes
	are	1,076.39 ft^2	100 m^2	1/100 hectare
	acre	43,560 ft^2	4,046.86 m^2	chain × furlong
ha	hectare	107,639 ft^2	0.01 km^2	2.47 acres
km^2	square kilometer	0.386102 mi^2	1,000,000 m^2	100 hectares
mi^2	square mile	27,878,400 ft^2	2.58999 km^2	640 acres
	tetrad	1.54441 mi^2	4 km^2	a square 2 × 2 km
	hectad	38.6102 mi^2	100 km^2	a square 10 × 10 km
	myriad	3,861.02 mi^2	10,000 km^2	a square 100 × 100 km
m^2	square meter	10.7639 ft^2	10,000 cm^2	1 centiare (ca)
yd^2	square yard	9 ft^2	0.836127 m^2	
ft^2, □	square foot	144 in^2	0.092903 m^2	
b	barn	1.55×10^{-24} in^2	10^{-28} m^2	100 square femtometers

VOLUME

Symbol	Unit	Equivalent	Equivalent	Notes
m^3	cubic meter	264.172 US gal	1,000,000 cm^3	1 stère, 1 kiloliter
L, l, ℓ	liter	1.05669 US qt	1000 mL	1 cubic decimeter
mL	milliliter	0.0610237 cu in	0.001 L	1 cm^3
AF	acre foot	43,560 cu ft	1,233.48 m^3	chain × furlong × foot
BF	board foot	144 cu in	2,359.73 cm^3	foot × foot × inch
imp gal	imperial gallon	277.419 cu in	4.54609 L	4 imp qt
imp qt	imperial quart	69.3547 cu in	1.13652 L	2 imp pt
imp pt	imperial pint	34.6774 cu in	0.56826 L	20 imp fl oz
imp fl oz	imperial fluid ounce	1.73387 cu in	28.4131 mL	1.6 imp tbsp
imp tbsp	imperial tablespoon	1.08367 cu in	17.7582 mL	3 imp tsp
imp tsp	imperial teaspoon	0.361225 cu in	5.91939 mL	
US gal	US gallon	231 cu in	3.78541 L	4 US qt
US qt	US quart	57.75 cu in	0.94635 L	2 US pt
US pt	US pint	28.875 cu in	0.47317 L	16 US fl oz
c	cup	14.4375 cu in	236.588 mL	16 US tbsp
US fl oz	US fluid ounce	1.80469 cu in	29.5735 mL	2 US tbsp
US tbsp	US tablespoon	0.902344 cu in	14.7868 mL	3 US tsp
US tsp	US teaspoon	0.300781 cu in	4.92892 mL	
cu yd	cubic yard	27 cu ft	0.764555 m^3	
cu ft	cubic foot	1728 cu in	0.0283168 m^3	
cu in	cubic inch	0.000578704 cu ft	16.3871 cm^3	1.10823 US tbsp
cm^3, cc	cubic centimeter	0.0610237 cu in	1 mL	1/1,000,000 m^3

MASS

Symbol	Unit	Equivalent	Equivalent	Notes
t	metric ton, tonne	2,204.62 lb	1,000 kg	1 megagram (Mg)
kg	kilogram	2.20462 lb	1,000 g	~1 L of H_2O at 4°C
g	gram	0.035274 oz	0.001 kg	
st	stone	14 lb	6.35029 kg	
lb, lb_m, #	pound; pound-mass	16 oz	0.453592 kg	
oz	ounce	0.911458 oz t	28.3495 g	1/16 lb
ozt	troy ounce	1.09714 oz	31.1035 g	1/12 troy pound
	carat	0.00705479 oz	0.2 g	4 jeweller's grains
u	atomic mass unit		1.66×10^{-27} kg	1/12 the mass of a carbon-12 atom

SPEED

Symbol	Unit	Equivalent	Equivalent	Equivalent
m/s, $m \cdot s^{-1}$	meter per second	2.23694 mph	3.6 km/h	1.94384 kn
km/h, $km \cdot h^{-1}$, kph	kilometer per hour	0.621371 mph	0.27 m/s	0.539957 kn
mph, mi/h	mile per hour	1.46667 ft/s	1.60934 km/h	0.868976 kn
ft/s	foot per second	0.681818 mph	1.09728 km/h	0.592484 kn
kn	knot	1.15078 mph	1.852 km/h	

* Usage of the word "pound" often conflates mass and weight. The **pound-force** (a measure of weight) corresponds to the gravitational force (32.174 ft/s²) exerted on a mass of one avoirdupois pound (**pound-mass**) at the surface of Earth. "Pound" may also refer to the unit of currency originating in Britain (£), or basis weight, a measure of mass per unit of area for paper and fabric.

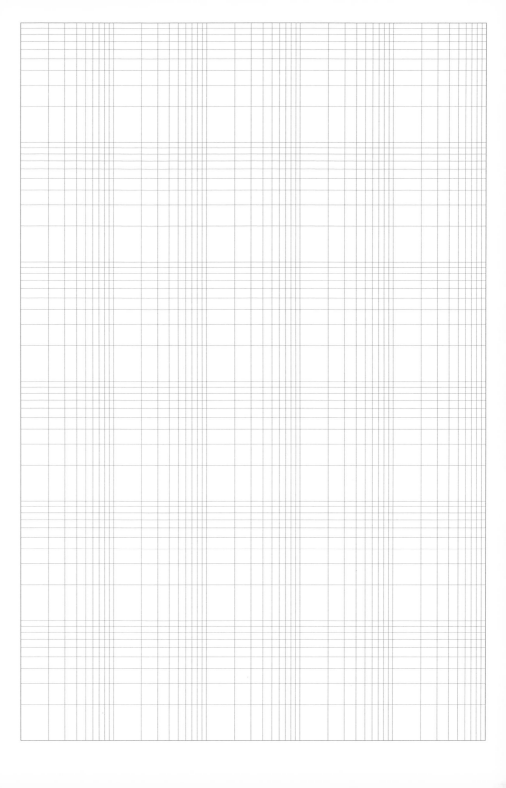

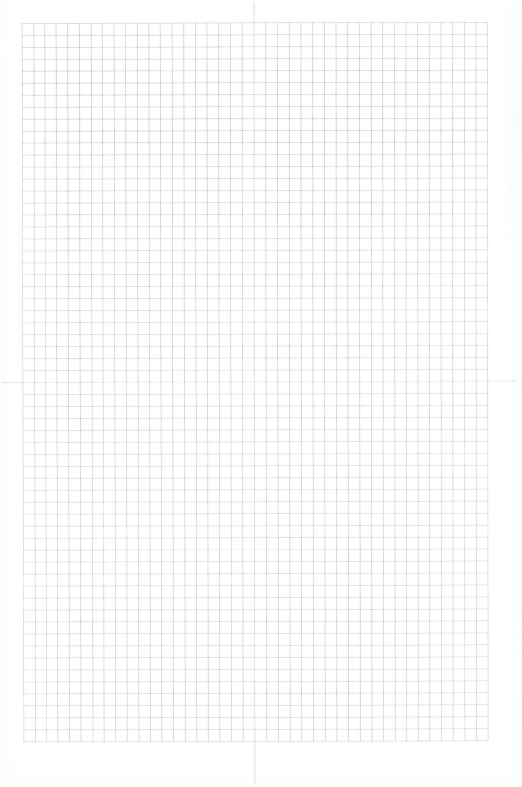

A number F_n in the **Fibonacci sequence** is defined by the recurrence relation $F_n = F_{n-1} + F_{n-2}$ where $F_1 = 0, F_2 = 1$.

$$0, 1, 1, 2, 3, 5, 8, 13, 21, 34, 55, 89, 144, 233, 377, 610, 987, 1597, 2584, 4181, 6765, 10946, \ldots$$

The **golden ratio** is approximated by $\dfrac{F_n}{F_{n-1}}$ where F_n is any number in the sequence and F_{n-1} is the preceding number.

$$\frac{1}{1} = 1 \quad \frac{2}{1} = 2 \quad \frac{3}{2} = 1.5 \quad \frac{5}{3} = 1.\overline{6} \quad \frac{8}{5} = 1.6 \quad \frac{13}{8} = 1.625 \quad \frac{21}{13} = 1.61538 \quad \frac{34}{21} = 1.61905 \quad \frac{55}{34} = 1.61765$$

$$\ldots \frac{10946}{6765} = 1.61803 \quad \approx \quad \varphi = 1.618\,033\,988\,749\,894\,848\,204\,586\,834\,365\,638\,117\,720 \ldots$$

Arranging squares of width F_n for several values of n approximates a **golden rectangle**. Larger values yield a more accurate figure. A golden rectangle is a rectangle with sides a and b, such that a is to b as b is to $a-b$:

$$\frac{a}{b} = \frac{b}{a-b} = \varphi$$

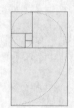
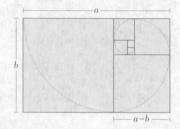

Because the Fibonacci sequence is a linear recurrence with constant coefficients, it has a closed-form solution, known as **Binet's formula**:

$$F_n = \frac{\varphi^n - \psi^n}{\varphi - \psi} = \frac{\varphi^n - \psi^n}{\sqrt{5}}$$

$$\text{where} \quad \varphi = \frac{1+\sqrt{5}}{2}$$

$$\approx 1.61803 \quad \text{(the golden ratio)}$$

$$\text{and} \quad \psi = \frac{1-\sqrt{5}}{2} = 1-\varphi = \frac{-1}{\varphi}$$

$$\approx -0.61803 \quad \text{(the inverse golden ratio)}$$

A pentagram contains ten isosceles triangles: five acute and five obtuse. In each, the ratio of the longer side to the shorter side is φ. The acute triangles are called **golden triangles**; the obtuse triangles are called **golden gnomons**.

$$\frac{d}{c} = \frac{f}{e} = \varphi$$

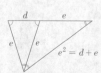

$$e^2 = d + e$$

golden triangle   golden gnomon

Ptolemy's theorem relates the side length m and chord length n of a regular pentagon inscribed in a circle:

$$n \cdot n = m \cdot m + n \cdot m$$

$$n^2 = m^2 + nm$$

$$\frac{n}{m} = \frac{1+\sqrt{5}}{2} = \varphi$$

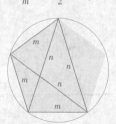

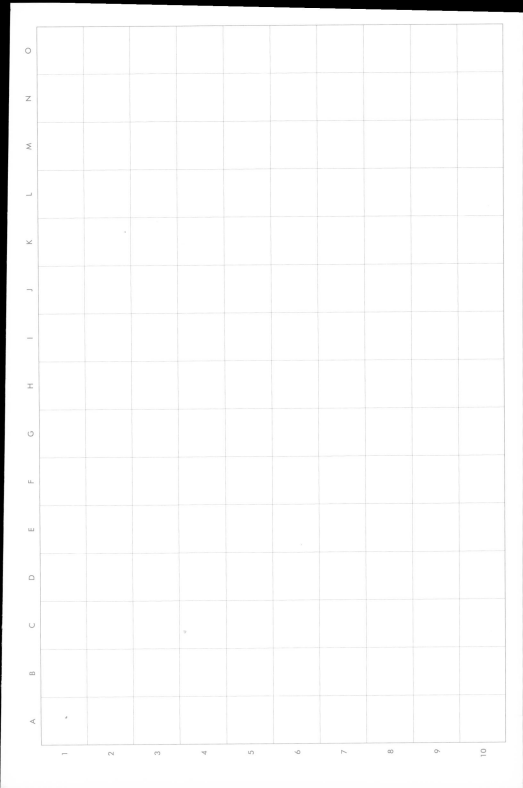